Table of Contents

Number and Place Value

Geometry

Fundamental Operations

Measurement

Fractions

Statistics

AR = Augmented Realty Page

Augmented Reality: How it Works

Head to the Apple App Store and download our app called Year 3 Maths Smartbooks

Use any device running ios 11.0 or above

App

Demo Video

Augmented Reality is a new and exciting **interactive experience** where virtual objects are placed in the real world right in front of you. There will be 3D characters asking you questions, fun card games with celebrating wizards, videos, and lots more.

Counting in Multiples

1. Find the way to the castle by writing the missing multiples of 4.

4 → ☐ → 12 → ☐ → 20 →

2. Colour the box **green** if the number is a multiple of 8, **red** if it is a multiple of 100 and do nothing if it's neither .

700	64	300	40	900	32	85
38	200	108	72	80	56	600

3. Tommy has 5 baskets of carrots. If each basket has 50 carrots, how many carrots does he have in all?

He has ☐ carrots in all.

48	57	30	8	24	43

4. What cards are multiples of 4 and 8?

☐

5. What two cards add together to make a multiple of 50

☐

"I can count in multiples of 4, 8, 50, and 100."

1

Augmented Reality Page

1) **Cut out** the cards

2) Go to **Chapter 1 - Multiples**

3) **Make the number** on the screen with the cards

4) **Move your phone** over the cards

10 and 100 More or Less of a Number

1. Fill in the table below. The first row has been done for you.

Number	10 Less	10 More	100 Less	100 More
120	110	130	20	220
375				
540				
680				

2. Colour Maggie's statement **green** if it is true or **red** if it is false.

100 less than 437 is greater than 400

100 more than 511 is greater than 700

10 more than 961 is the same as 971

3. Maggie's broomstick has 100 less than 206 sticks. This morning, 10 more sticks broke. How many sticks are left on Maggie's broomstick?

Maggie's broomstick has [   ] sticks left.

"I can find 10 and 100 more or less of a number."

Place Value and Value

LET US FIND THE PLACE VALUE AND VALUE OF A NUMBER

1. Help the rabbits find their hat by identifying how many hundreds they have.

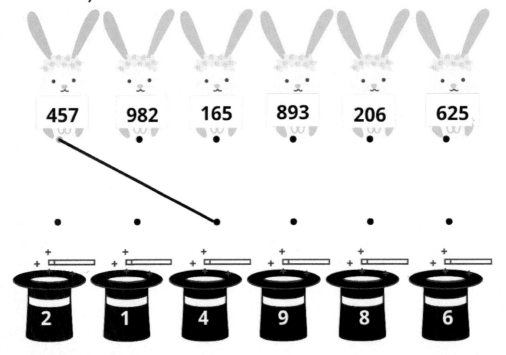

2. What is the place value and value of the underlined digit.

Number	Place Value	Value
3<u>2</u>4		
48<u>5</u>		
<u>5</u>92		
<u>7</u>16		

3. Write the number being described by Kimmy, the witch.

9 ones, 6 tens, 2 hundreds _____

7 hundreds, 8 tens, 3 ones _____

4 tens, 5 hundreds, 6 ones _____

4. Partition the numbers into hundreds, tens, and ones. The first one has been done for you.

658 = [600] + [50] + [8]

217 = [ ] + [ ] + [ ]

934 = [ ] + [ ] + [ ]

562 = [ ] + [ ] + [ ]

Use the magic cards to do the tasks.

5. What is the biggest 3-digit number that can be formed with 5 in the ones place?

[ ]

6. What is the smallest 3-digit number that can be formed with 3 in the tens place?

[ ]

"*I can tell the place value and value of a number.*"

Augmented Reality Page

PLACE VALUE MAGIC CARDS

1) **Cut out** the cards
2) Go to **Chapter 1 - Place Value**
3) **Make the number** on the screen with the cards
4) **Move your phone** over the cards

Place Value

3

Place Value

5

Place Value

7

Comparing and Ordering Numbers

1. Cross (X) the rabbit which holds the smallest number and tick (✓) the rabbit which holds the biggest number.

| 329 | 145 | 908 | 623 | 809 |

2. Use >, < , and = to compare the numbers. The first one is done for you.

580 __<__ 850   273 _____237   899 _____901

496 _____ 469   5+11 _____ 15+1   7+5 _____9-6

3. Arrange their heights from shortest to tallest.

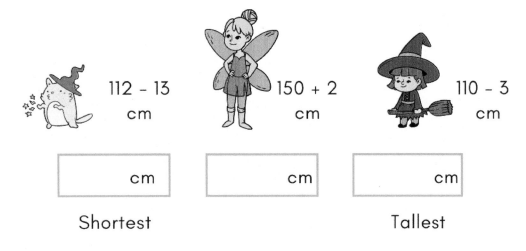

112 – 13 cm   150 + 2 cm   110 – 3 cm

| cm | cm | cm |

Shortest   Tallest

"I can compare and order numbers."

Augmented Reality Page

1) Cut out the cards on this page

2) Go to **Chapter 1 - Ordering and comparing**

3) Place the **> < =** cards **between the numbers** on the next page

4) Move your phone over the cards

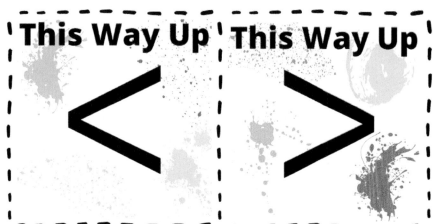

Don't cut out

273

Place card here

237

899

Place card here

901

Don't cut out

417

Place card
here

471

221

Place card
here

213

Don't cut out

5+7   Place card here   2+9

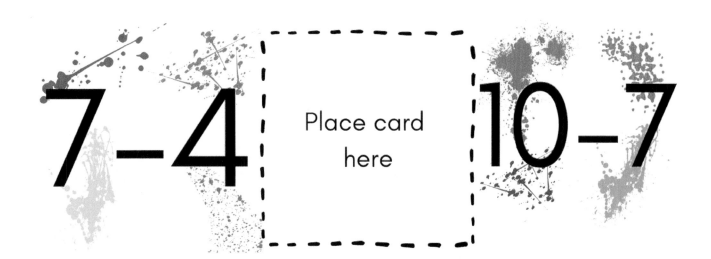

7−4   Place card here   10−7

 # Representing Numbers

LET US REPRESENT NUMBERS IN DIFFERENT WAYS

1. An election for the school head boy is conducted. The number of votes for Nick is shown in the tally below. How many people voted for Nick?

```
votes
```

2. John measures his eraser. How long is his eraser?

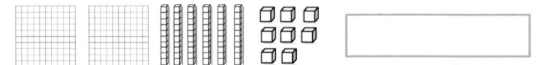

```
cm
```

3. What number is being represented by the grids?

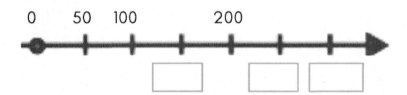

4. Write the missing numbers on the number line.

5. I am a number that has 4 tens, 8 ones, and 6 hundreds. What number am I?

"I can represent number indifferent ways."

Reading and Writing Numbers

1. Draw a line to match the numbers with the correct written words.

457	•	•	three hundred forty-six
932	•	•	four hundred fifty-seven
346	•	•	six hundred eighty-one
681	•	•	nine hundred thirty-two

2. Write these numbers in words.

649 →
138 →
725 →

3. Draw ☺ if the statement is correct or ☹ if it is wrong.

_____ Two hundred and seventy-two is written as 227.

_____ Five hundred and four is written as 504.

_____ 846 is written as eight hundred and fourty-six in words.

4. Leila's sister is six years older than her. If her sister is twenty years old now, how old is Leila? Write your answer in words.

Hello! I am _____ years old.

"*I can read and write numbers in numerals and words.*"

Solving Number Problems

1. Jake sold 400 magic wands yesterday. Today, he sold 11 wands less than yesterday. How many wands did he sell today?

"I sold ⬚ wands today."

2. Angela, Dave, and James measured their weight. Angela weighed 22 kg, Dave weighed 21 kg, and James weighed 30 kg. What do they weigh together?

" ⬚ kg"

3. Ron has 548 magic hats in his shop. 100 more hats were delivered. How many magic hats does he have now? Write your answer in words.

"I have ⬚ hats."

4. Fill in the boxes using >, <, = .

10 less than 585	100 more than 380
100 more than 702	10 less than 812
64 + 12	80 – 19

5. Gail has 6 boxes containing 100 apples each. How many apples does she have in all?

"I have _____ apples."

Use the magic cards to do the following tasks.

6. Create the biggest 3-digit number that has 5 tens.

7. Create the smallest 3-digit number that has 4 ones.

"I can solve problems involving numbers."

14

CHAPTER TEST

1. Circle the numbers that are multiples of 50 but not multiples of 100.

100   **250**   **300**   **350**   **450**   **500**   **750**   **800**

2. Write the correct numbers in the boxes.

100 more than 763

100 less than 690

3. How would you describe 435? Colour your answer.

400 hundreds, 30 tens, 5 ones

4 hundreds, 3 tens, 5 ones

4. What is the value of 7 in the following numbers?

780 | 700

279 |

127 |

724 |

5. Compare the numbers using >, <, =.

700 + 50 ☐ 750 + 0   900 + 25 ☐ 400 + 72

300 + 60 ☐ 570 + 2   150 + 8 ☐ 100 + 58

620 + 5 ☐ 420 + 5   540 + 100 ☐ 750 – 100

6. Check the box if the numbers are arranged from smallest to biggest, or cross if arranged from biggest to smallest.

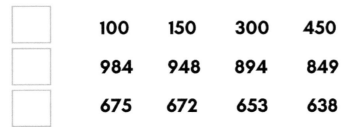

	100	150	300	450
	984	948	894	849
	675	672	653	638

7. Arrange the numbers from smallest to biggest. Write your answers in the hat.

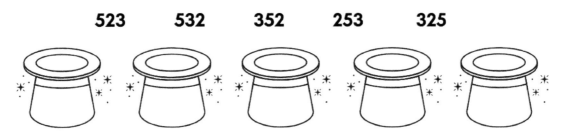

523   532   352   253   325

8. Write the numbers in being represented by the grids.

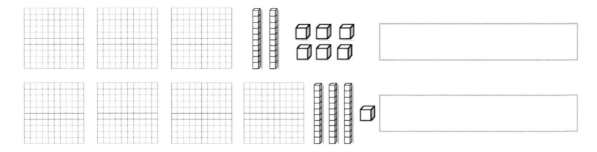

9. Match the numeral to its correct word.

243 •   • six hundred and thirty-two

528 •   • nine hundred and seven

907 •   • five hundred and twenty-eight

165 •   • two hundred and forty-three

632 •   • one hundred and sixty-five

Augmented Reality Page

1) Go to **Chapter 2** ➔ **Challenge** in the app
2) **Move your phone** over the cards below

Number and Place Value

Question

1

Number and Place Value

Answer

1

Number and Place Value

Question

2

Number and Place Value

Answer

2

Number and Place Value

Question

3

Number and Place Value

Answer

3

CERTIFICATE

THIS IS PRESENTED TO

For learning about Numbers and Place Value

BELIEVE IN YOURSELF

Adding Mentally

LET US ADD NUMBERS IN OUR HEAD

1. Complete the number pyramid. Add the following numbers in your head. Write your answers in the box above.

780	4

320	500

520	60

135	400

2. Write a number in each box to make the equation correct.

$260 + \boxed{} = 560$ $720 + \boxed{} = 728$

$\boxed{} + 90 = 695$ $\boxed{} + 800 = 864$

3. What number is formed when you add three hundred and ninety-four to two hundred?

4. Maggie has five magic cards. She wants to know what are the 3 numbers that she can add to get 180. Can you help her circle those three cards?

"I can add numbers mentally."

Augmented Reality Page

MENTAL ADDITION MAGIC CARDS

1) **Cut out** the cards

2) Go to **Chapter 2 - Mental Addition** in the app

3) **Make the number** on the screen with the cards

4) **Move your phone** over the cards

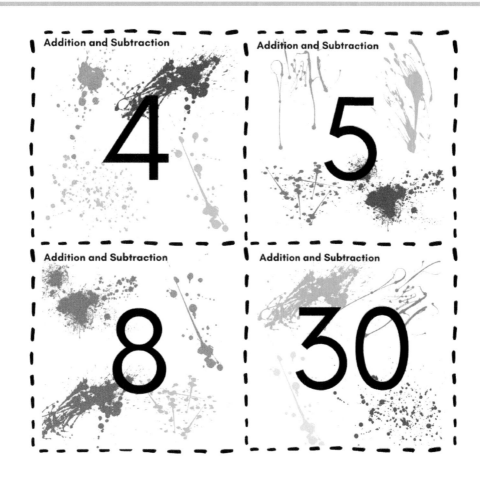

Addition and Subtraction 111	Addition and Subtraction 213
Addition and Subtraction 221	Addition and Subtraction 417
Addition and Subtraction 427	Addition and Subtraction 500
Addition and Subtraction 100	Addition and Subtraction +

Subtracting Mentally

LET US SUBTRACT NUMBERS IN OUR HEAD

1. Decrease five hundred and seventy by two hundred and twenty. What is the number?

2. Complete the number puzzle by subtracting the numbers.

| 680 | 200 | | 750 | 5 | | 920 | 80 | | 487 | 380 |

3. Colour the hat according to the colour code.

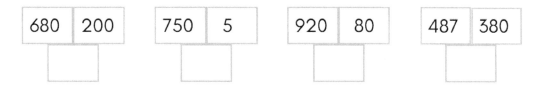

173 – 23   280 –110   965 – 60   829 – 329

500 – red   170 – green   150 – orange   905 – blue

4. Two numbers are subtracted and their difference is 572. Circle the two numbers.

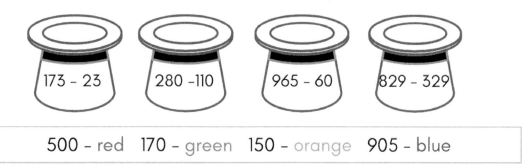

920   **282**   **772**   **472**   **200**

"I can subtract numbers mentally."

Augmented Reality Page

1) **Cut out** the card

2) Go to **Chapter 2 - Mental Subtraction** in the app

3) **Make the number** on the screen with the cards

4) **Move your phone** over the cards

Use the **number cards** from the **addition section**.

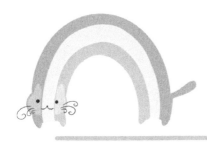

Written Addition

1. Add the following numbers.

600	248	536	190
+376	+ 453	+249	+ 627

345	568	365	752
+262	+ 402	+439	+143

2. Write numbers in the blue boxes to make the equation correct.

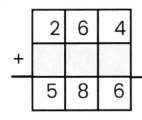

	2	6	4
+			
	5	8	6

+	1	2	0
	8	7	0

	5	3	9
+	2	4	3

3. Help Robert find the number treats. Yesterday, he bought 156 treats. The next day, his mom bought him 233 treats. How many treats does he have in total?

treats

"I can add 3-digit numbers using written methods."

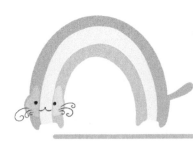

Written Subtraction

LET US SUBTRACT NUMBERS USING WRITTEN METHODS

1. Subtract the following numbers.

876 - 203	590 - 349	485 - 253	698 - 325	794 - 581

2. Colour the flower based on the colour code below.

Colour Code	
Green	220
Yellow	323
Red	326
Blue	425
Purple	208

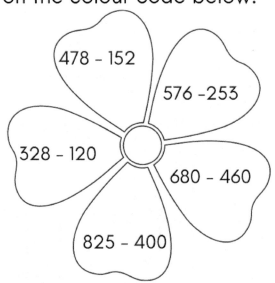

478 – 152

576 –253

328 – 120

680 – 460

825 – 400

3. How much taller is Castle A than Castle B?

Castle A

435 metres

Castle B

290 metres

metres

"I can subtract 3-digit numbers using written methods."

25

Augmented Reality Page

3 TIMES TABLES VIDEO PAGE

1) Go to **Chapter 2 ➜ 3 Times Tables in the app**

2) **Move your phone** over the picture below

3 Times Table Video

Augmented Reality Page

1) Go to **Chapter 2 ➔ 4 Times Tables in the app**

2) **Move your phone** over the picture below

Augmented Reality Page

1) Go to **Chapter 2 ➔ 8 Times Tables** in the app

2) **Move your phone** over the picture below

8 Times Table Video

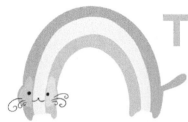

The 3, 4, and 8 Times Tables

LET US KNOW THE TIMES TABLES

1. Multiply the following numbers. Write your answers in the oval.

7 x 8	( )	3 x 9	( )	4 x 8	( )
4 x 10	( )	8 x 5	( )	3 x 4	( )
6 x 3	( )	7 x 4	( )	9 x 4	( )

2. Circle all the magic cards that are in the 8 times table.

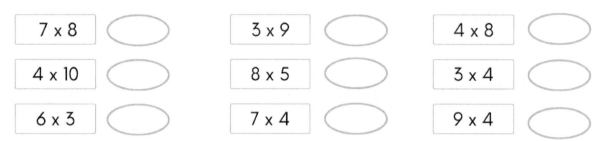

64   75   56   45   32   80

3. Box the numbers in this list that divide exactly by four.

22   16   18   28   32   13   8   20   36

4. Fill in the blanks with the correct number.

56 ÷ 8 = [ ]   20 ÷ [ ] = 5   [ ] ÷ 3 = 8

5. Jimmy loves to collect bones. He collected 63 bones in one week. How many bones did he equally collect each day?

[   ] bones

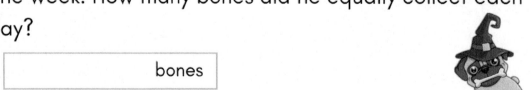

"I can tell the 3, 4, and 8 times tables."

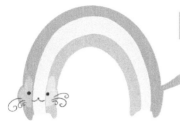

Multiplying and Dividing Numbers

LETS USE TIMES TABLES FACTS

1. Test your magic of speed by solving these equations correctly.

2 x 3 x 5		7 x 2 x 2		9 x 1 x 2	
6 x 50		8 x 50		5 x 3 x 0	
20 x 5		34 x 6		25 x 8	

2. Fix the wands by dividing the following numbers correctly. Write your answer in the star.

12 ÷ 6   72 ÷ 9   450 ÷ 5

3. Leila had 160 sweets. She divided them equally with her 8 friends. How many sweets did each friend receive?

Answer: [   ] candies

"*I can multiply and divide numbers using times tables.*"

Estimating and Checking

LET US LEARN THE USE OF INVERSE OPERATIONS

1. Estimate the answer to the nearest hundred. The first one is done for you.

219	200	670		442	
+ 360	400	- 238		+ 590	
	600				

2. Alice calculated **445 - 100 = 345**. Write the inverse calculation to prove that she is correct.

3. Write a division sentence for every multiplication sentence.

11 x 8 = 88   [ ] ÷ [ ] = [ ]

20 x 7 = 140   [ ] ÷ [ ] = [ ]

15 x 4 = 60   [ ] ÷ [ ] = [ ]

4. Rick divided 90 pieces of sweets equally into 10 bags. He said: "Each bag has 11 sweets." Is he correct? Prove your answer by writing the inverse calculation.

"I can estimate the answer to a calculation and check the answer using inverse operation."

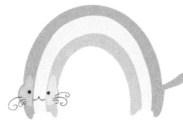

Solving Computation Problems

LET US SOLVE CALCULATION PROBLEMS

1. There are 215 Math books and 347 Science books in the library. How many Math and Science books are there in all?

books

2. There are 457 pages in Kyla's book. She has already read 289 pages. How many more pages does she need to read?

pages

3. John has 185 marbles. 95 marbles are red and the rest are green. How many marbles are green?

marbles

4. What number will you get if you add the difference between 815 and 638 to 756?

5. A class has 35 students. They are divided into 5 groups. How many students are there in each group?

students

6. Jim drinks 2 litres of water everyday. How many litres of water will he drink in five weeks?

| litres |

7. Jack spends 45 minutes each day jogging in a nearby park. How many minutes does he spend jogging for 4 days?

| minutes |

8. Anna baked 35 cookies. After dividing the cookies equally among 3 children, she had 11 cookies left. How many cookies did each child get?

| cookies |

9. Use the digits 3, 8, and 5 to form the biggest and the smallest 3-digit number. Find their difference.

biggest 3-digit number

smallest 3-digit number

difference

CHAPTER TEST

1. Draw a line from the equation to its correct answer.

340 + 300   •   •   709

930 – 220   •   •   230

680 – 450   •   •   672

542 + 130   •   •   710

769 – 60   •   •   640

2. Perform the indicated operation.

530	285	406	623	768
+ 259	+ 174	+ 583	– 326	– 158

3. Circle the multiples of the given number.

3	9	10	13	15	19
4	7	8	14	18	20
8	18	22	24	28	32

4. Use the times table to find the answer.

 25 x 8 =   120 ÷ 2 =

60 x 4 =   64 ÷ 4 =

48 x 3 =   90 ÷ 3 =

5. Estimate the answer to the nearest hundred.

498		375		663	
− 180		+ 439		− 349	

6. Write the inverse equation to check the answer. If the answer is correct, put a check in the circle. If it is wrong, put a cross.

569 + 219 = 788

925 − 545 = 300

10 x 8 = 80

144 ÷ 4 = 35

7. Lea sold 125 pencils. If she and her brother sold a total of 380 pencils, how many pencils did her brother sell?

pencils

8. Leo has 40 toy cars. He donated them equally to 8 kids. How many toy cars did each kid receive?

toy cars

9. Kimmy jogs 30 minutes a day. How many minutes did she jog for 5 days?

minutes

35

Augmented Reality Page

CHALLENGE QUESTIONS

1) Go to **Chapter 2 ➜ Challenge** in the app
2) **Move your phone** over the cards below

Fundamental Operations

Question

1

Fundamental Operations

Answer

1

Don't cut out

Fundamental Operations

Question

2

Fundamental Operations

Answer

2

Fundamental Operations

Question

3

Fundamental Operations

Answer

3

CERTIFICATE

THIS IS PRESENTED TO

○————————————————○

For learning about Fundamental Operations

BELIEVE IN YOURSELF

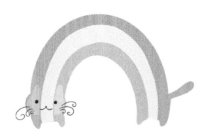

Counting in Tenths

1. Label the fractions.

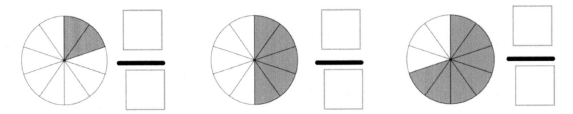

2. Shade $\frac{3}{10}$ of the rectangle and shade $\frac{9}{10}$ of the circle.

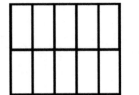 

3. Write the five missing fractions in the number line.

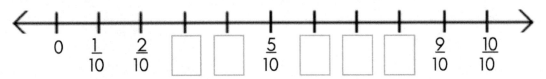

4. What fraction of these shapes are circles?

"I can count using tenths."

38

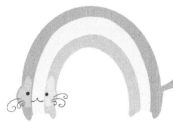

Equivalent Fractions

LET US RECOGNIZE EQUIVALENT FRACTIONS

1. Draw the parts of the second pizza to make it equivalent to the first pizza. Write the fraction for each pizza in the box.

   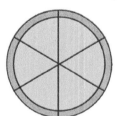

Shade the figures to make equivalent fractions. Write the fraction for each shape in the box.

2.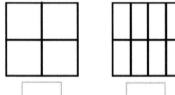

3.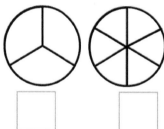

4. Circle the fractions that are equivalent to $\frac{2}{8}$.

$\frac{4}{16}$ $\frac{3}{9}$ $\frac{2}{3}$ $\frac{1}{4}$ $\frac{6}{24}$ $\frac{5}{20}$ $\frac{8}{10}$

5. State three fractions that are equivalent to $\frac{3}{6}$ and have a denominator less than 9?

Comparing and Ordering Fractions

LET US COMPARE AND ORDER FRACTIONS

1. Find the smallest and largest fractions. Colour the smallest fraction yellow and the largest green.

$$\frac{4}{8} \qquad \frac{5}{8} \qquad \frac{2}{8} \qquad \frac{7}{8} \qquad \frac{6}{8}$$

2. Use >, <, = to compare the fractions.

$$\frac{4}{15} \;\square\; \frac{14}{15} \qquad \frac{5}{6} \;\square\; \frac{3}{6} \qquad \frac{9}{12} \;\square\; \frac{9}{12}$$

$$\frac{1}{7} \;\square\; \frac{1}{8} \qquad \frac{1}{6} \;\square\; \frac{1}{4} \qquad \frac{1}{2} \;\square\; \frac{1}{5}$$

3. Arrange these fractions from smallest to biggest.

$$\frac{4}{9} \qquad \frac{3}{9} \qquad \frac{8}{9} \qquad \frac{6}{9} \qquad \frac{1}{9}$$

smallest ⬜ ⬜ ⬜ ⬜ ⬜ biggest

4. Arrange these fractions from biggest to smallest.

$$\frac{1}{12} \qquad \frac{1}{8} \qquad \frac{1}{9} \qquad \frac{1}{6} \qquad \frac{1}{3}$$

biggest ⬜ ⬜ ⬜ ⬜ ⬜ smallest

5. Cecil bought a pie for Dave, Sam, and Tom. Dave ate $\frac{3}{8}$ of the pie. Sam ate $\frac{1}{8}$ and Tom ate $\frac{4}{8}$ of the pie. Who ate the largest bit of pie?

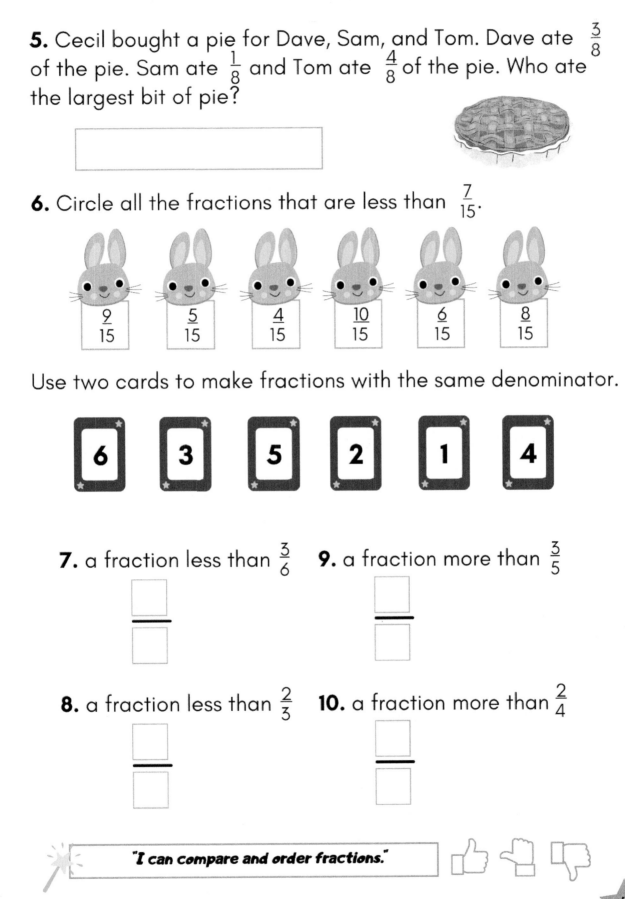

6. Circle all the fractions that are less than $\frac{7}{15}$.

| $\frac{9}{15}$ | $\frac{5}{15}$ | $\frac{4}{15}$ | $\frac{10}{15}$ | $\frac{6}{15}$ | $\frac{8}{15}$ |

Use two cards to make fractions with the same denominator.

| 6 | 3 | 5 | 2 | 1 | 4 |

7. a fraction less than $\frac{3}{6}$

9. a fraction more than $\frac{3}{5}$

8. a fraction less than $\frac{2}{3}$

10. a fraction more than $\frac{2}{4}$

"I can compare and order fractions."

Adding and Subtracting Fractions

LET US ADD AND SUBTRACT FRACTIONS

Add/Subtract the fractions. Shade the last figure to represent your answer and write the fraction for it.

1. 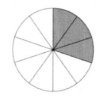 + 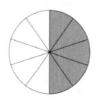 =

2. 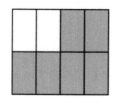 - 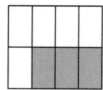 =

3. Find the sum of these fractions.

$$\frac{3}{16} + \frac{2}{16} = \frac{\square}{\square} \qquad \frac{2}{7} + \frac{5}{7} = \frac{\square}{\square} \qquad \frac{8}{13} + \frac{4}{13} = \frac{\square}{\square}$$

4. Find the difference of these fractions.

$$\frac{15}{20} - \frac{9}{20} = \frac{\square}{\square} \qquad \frac{9}{10} - \frac{4}{10} = \frac{\square}{\square} \qquad \frac{14}{15} - \frac{7}{15} = \frac{\square}{\square}$$

5. Fill in the missing fraction.

$$\frac{4}{9} + \frac{\square}{\square} = \frac{9}{9} \qquad \frac{\square}{\square} + \frac{8}{14} = \frac{10}{14} \qquad \frac{5}{6} - \frac{\square}{\square} = \frac{1}{6}$$

6. What is seven-eights minus three-eights?

7. What is the answer in $\frac{3}{9} + \frac{4}{9} - \frac{5}{9}$?

8. What fraction should be added to $\frac{2}{7}$ to make a whole?

9. Kate read $\frac{2}{5}$ of her book at night. The next morning she reads the same amount. What fraction has she got left ?

10. Kat and three of her children bought a pizza and shared it equally among themselves. They divided the pizza into 8 slices. What fraction of the pizza was eaten by the three children?

11. What fraction of the pizza was eaten by Mum?

12. Annie saves $\frac{3}{10}$ of her allowance and spends the rest. What fraction of her allowance is used for spendings?

"I can add and subtract fractions."

Augmented Reality Page

ADDING FRACTIONS

1) **Cut out** the cards

2) Go to **Chapter 3 - Adding Fractions** in the app

3) **Make the number** on the screen with the cards

4) **Move your phone** over the cards

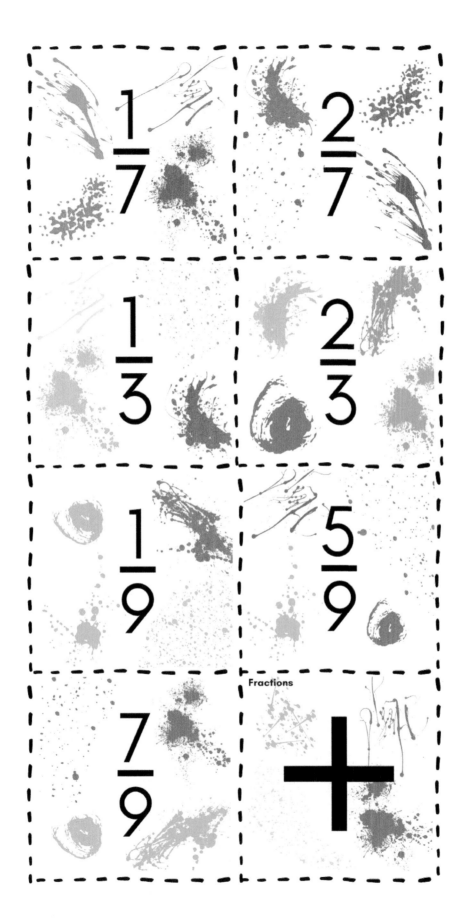

$\dfrac{1}{7}$ $\dfrac{2}{7}$

$\dfrac{1}{3}$ $\dfrac{2}{3}$

$\dfrac{1}{9}$ $\dfrac{5}{9}$

$\dfrac{7}{9}$ **+**

Fractions

Augmented Reality Page

1) **Cut out** the card

2) Go to **Chapter 2 - Subtracting Fractions** in the app

3) **Make the number** on the screen with the cards

4) **Move your phone** over the cards

Use the previous addition faction cards for the numbers

Fractions
This Way Up

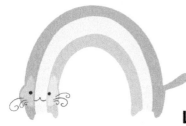

Unit and Non-Unit Fractions

LET US LEARN UNIT AND NON-UNIT FRACTIONS

1. Label the fractions.

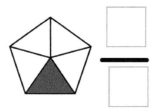 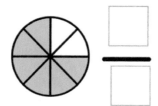 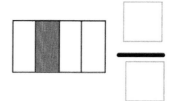

2. Box $\frac{2}{8}$ of the cats.

3. Circle the unit fractions and cross the non-unit fractions.

$$\frac{1}{16} \qquad \frac{2}{3} \qquad \frac{3}{5} \qquad \frac{1}{4} \qquad \frac{6}{8} \qquad \frac{1}{7} \qquad \frac{1}{10}$$

4. Gary has 20 candies. He shared $\frac{3}{5}$ of them with his friends. How many candies did his friends receive?

candies

5. Ivy has 80 flowers. She gave $\frac{1}{8}$ of it to her mom. How many roses did her mom receive?

roses

6. Box $\frac{3}{4}$ of the apples.

7. Solve the following.

$\frac{1}{2}$ of 12 = ☐ $\frac{1}{6}$ of 48 = ☐ $\frac{2}{5}$ of 45= ☐

$\frac{1}{3}$ of 36 = ☐ $\frac{3}{4}$ of 20 = ☐ $\frac{2}{7}$ of 49= ☐

8. What is $\frac{3}{4}$ of 40? Circle the correct answer.

10   **12**   **16**   **20**   **25**   **30**   **35**   **38**

9. What is two-thirds of twenty-seven?

☐

10. Luke and Jane ask a nurse to measure their height. Luke is 120 cm tall and Jane is $\frac{3}{4}$ as tall as Luke. How tall is Jane?

☐ cm

11. Liz spent $\frac{2}{5}$ of her savings. If she had £15, how much is now left in her savings?

£ ☐

Solving Fraction Problems

LET US SOLVE FRACTION PROBLEMS

1. Aunt bought 1 kilogram of sugar. She used $\frac{1}{3}$ of it to bake a cake. What fraction of the sugar was left?

2. Ken had 30 marbles. He gave $\frac{2}{3}$ of the marbles to his friends. How many marbles were given to his friends?

_____ marbles

3. Twenty children attended the party. $\frac{3}{5}$ are boys and the rest are girls. How many girls attended the party?

_____ girls

4. In a box of 24 doughnuts, $\frac{3}{6}$ are chocolate, $\frac{2}{6}$ are strawberry, and the rest are vanilla. How many doughnuts are vanilla?

_____ doughnuts

5. Dad bought a large pizza with 10 slices. He ate $\frac{3}{8}$, Mum ate $\frac{2}{8}$, I ate $\frac{1}{8}$ and Liam ate the rest. Who ate the largest part?

6. Lizzie and Lara bought a ribbon for their project. Lizzie got $\frac{2}{5}$ of the ribbon and Lara got $\frac{1}{5}$ of the ribbon. What fraction of ribbon is left?

7. Three children ate $\frac{2}{10}$ of a cake each. What fraction of the cake do they eat in total?

8. What fraction of the cake was left?

9. In a cafe, $\frac{2}{6}$ of the tablecloths are yellow. If there are 12 yellow tablecloths, how many tablecloths are there in the cafe altogether?

tablecloths

"I can solve problems involving fractions"

CHAPTER TEST

1. What fraction of the animals are ducks?

2. What fraction of the animals are cats?

3. What fraction of the animals are frogs, dogs, and ducks?

4. Name the fraction for each figure.

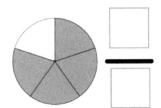 —  —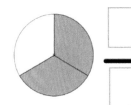

5. Pat has 12 bars of chocolate. She shared $\frac{2}{3}$ of it with her friends. How many bars of chocolate did her friends receive?

bars

6. Circle the fractions that are equivalent to $\frac{1}{4}$.

$$\frac{4}{16} \qquad \frac{2}{9} \qquad \frac{2}{8} \qquad \frac{1}{12} \qquad \frac{3}{12} \qquad \frac{4}{12} \qquad \frac{8}{16}$$

7. Use >, <, = to compare the fractions.

$\frac{1}{90}$ ☐ $\frac{1}{9}$ $\frac{1}{8}$ ☐ $\frac{1}{3}$ $\frac{9}{12}$ ☐ $\frac{9}{12}$

8. Write a fraction with the same denominator that is greater than $\frac{7}{13}$.

☐

9. Arrange the fractions from smallest to biggest.

$\frac{2}{13}$ $\frac{5}{13}$ $\frac{10}{13}$ $\frac{8}{13}$ $\frac{4}{13}$

smallest ☐ ☐ ☐ ☐ ☐ biggest

10. Fill in the missing fraction.

$\frac{6}{10} + \frac{\Box}{\Box} = \frac{9}{10}$ $\frac{\Box}{\Box} + \frac{5}{15} = \frac{13}{15}$ $\frac{7}{8} - \frac{\Box}{\Box} = \frac{4}{8}$

11. Leila ate $\frac{2}{6}$ of the pie and Ford ate $\frac{3}{6}$. What fraction of the pie did they eat altogether?

☐

12. Lara has $\frac{5}{6}$ kg of flour. She used $\frac{1}{6}$ kg when baking muffins. How many kilograms of flour were left?

☐ kg

Augmented Reality Page

1) Go to **Chapter 2 ➜ Challenge** in the app
2) **Move your phone** over the cards below

Don't cut out

Fractions

Question

1

Fractions

Answer

1

Don't cut out

CERTIFICATE

THIS IS PRESENTED TO

For learning about Fractions

BELIEVE IN YOURSELF

2D Shapes

LET US LEARN THE 2D SHAPES

What are the shapes of these objects.

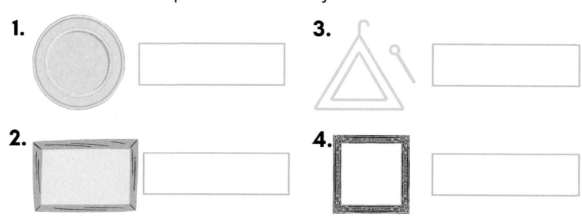

1.

3.

2.

4.

5. Colour the school bus according to the colour code on the box.

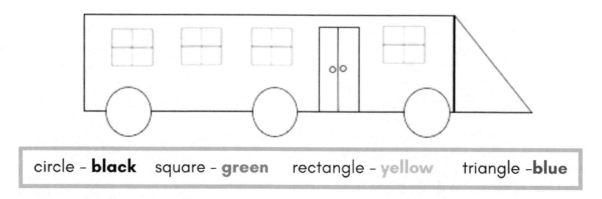

circle - **black**   square - **green**   rectangle - **yellow**   triangle –**blue**

6. Lizzie drew some shapes. Cross the quadrilaterals.

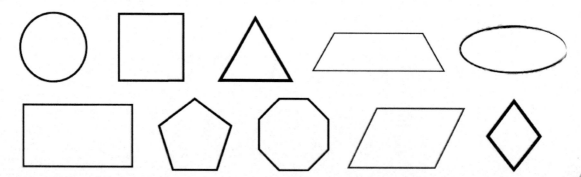

Complete the statement by writing the number of sides of each shape.

7. A square has ⬜ equal sides.

8. A triangle has ⬜ sides.

9. A pentagon has ⬜ sides.

10. An octagon has ⬜ sides.

11. A trapezoid has ⬜ sides.

Name the triangles. Say whether it is **equilateral**, **isosceles**, or **scalene**.

12.
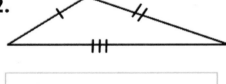

14.

13.
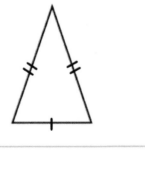

15.
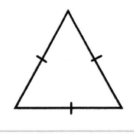

"*I can identify and draw 2D shapes.*"

Augmented Reality Page

3D SHAPES

1) Go to **Chapter 4 - 3D shapes** in the app

2) **Move your phone** over the shape cards

Cube

Sphere

Cone

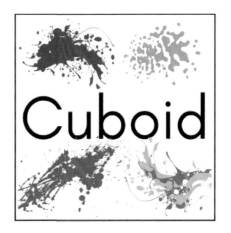

Cuboid

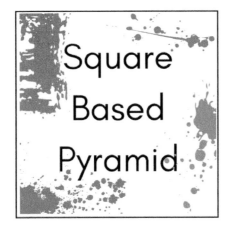

Square Based Pyramid

Cylinder

Tetrahedron

3D Shapes

Name the shape of the 3D objects.

1. [   ]

4.  [   ]

2. [   ]

5.  [   ]

3. 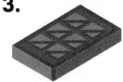 [   ]

6. [   ]

7. Circle the shapes that are prisms.

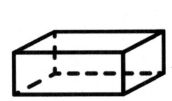   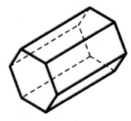

8. Draw a line from the 3D shape to its description.

Cylinder •   • It has no flat surfaces.

Sphere •   • It has two circular bases and a curved surface.

Cube •   • It has six square faces.

Count the edges, faces, and vertices of the 3D shapes.

9.

Edges _____

Faces _____

Vertices _____

11.

Edges _____

Faces _____

Vertices _____

10.

Edges _____

Faces _____

Vertices _____

12.

Edges _____

Faces _____

Vertices _____

Mary has two sets of cut-out shapes. She wants to create 3D shapes from these cut-outs. What 3D shapes can she create?

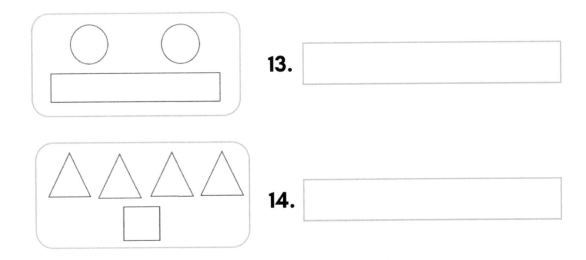

13. [_____]

14. [_____]

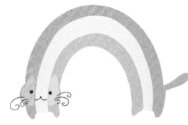

Recognizing Angles

LET US LEARN ABOUT ANGLES

Name the angles.

1.

2.

3.

4. Colour the shapes that have right angles.

5. Unscramble the jumbled letters to find out what kind of angle is being described.

This is an angle of exactly 90 degrees.   **G H R I T**

This is an angle of more than 90 degrees.   **S B O T U E**

This is an angle of fewer than 90 degrees.   **C T E U A**

6. How many right angles are there in a full turn?

right angles

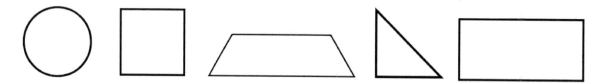

"I can recognize angles."

Lines

1. Count the vertical and horizontal lines in this figure.

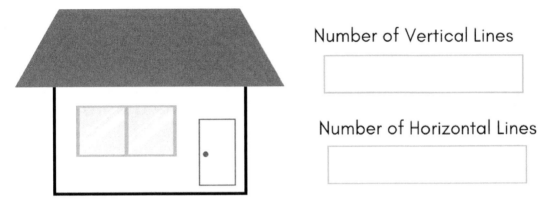

Number of Vertical Lines

Number of Horizontal Lines

2. Give an uppercase letter from the English alphabet that is composed of a horizontal line and two vertical lines.

Tell whether the lines are parallel or perpendicular.

3.

4.

5.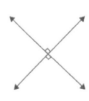

6. Colour the star green if the statement is correct. Colour it red if the statement is wrong.

 Parallel lines can meet eventually.

 Perpendicular lines always make a 90-degree angle.

Look at the figure.

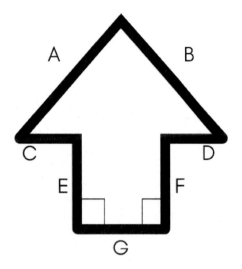

7. Which side is parallel to side E?

8. Which side is perpendicular to side F?

9. Is side A and side B parallel, yes or no?

Look at the grid and do the tasks.

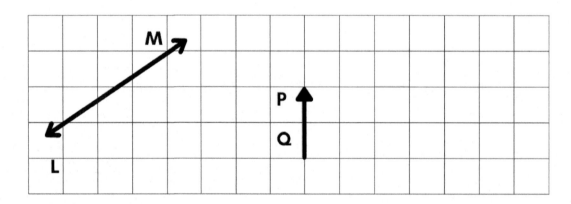

10. Draw a line parallel to line LM and name it as line TU.

11. Draw a line perpendicular to PQ and name it as line QR.

"I can identify and draw vertical, horizontal, parallel, and perpendicular lines.."

CHAPTER TEST

1. Solve the puzzle.

Across

1. Shapes that have four sides.

4. It has three sides.

5. Shape with no corners or edges.

Down

2. It has four sides but two sides are longer.

3. It has four equal sides.

2. Draw a line from the object to its shape.

cylinder   pyramid   cone   cube   sphere

3. Put a check in the circle if the statement is true or cross if it is wrong.

○ A circle is a 3D shape.

○ A cone is composed of a circular base and an apex.

○ A shape with 6 square faces is called a pyramid.

4. Classify the angles below into acute, right, and obtuse. Write the letter of the angle in its proper column.

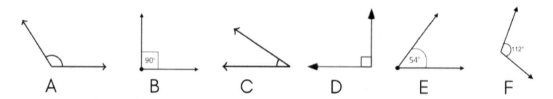

A   B   C   D   E   F

Acute	Right	Obtuse

5. Do the object shows parallel or perpendicular lines?

Augmented Reality Page

1) Go to **Chapter 4 - Challenge** in the app
2) Move your phone over the cards below

Don't cut out

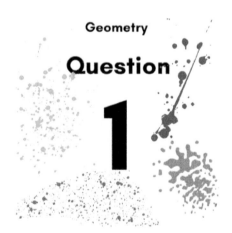

Geometry

Question

1

Geometry

Answer

1

Don't cut out

Geometry

Question

2

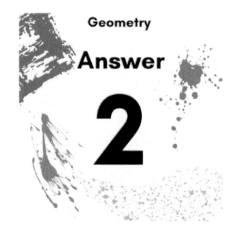

Geometry

Answer

2

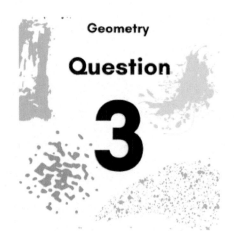

Geometry

Question

3

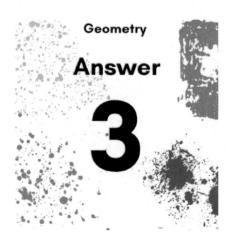

Geometry

Answer

3

CERTIFICATE

THIS IS PRESENTED TO

For learning about Geometry

BELIEVE IN YOURSELF

Length, Mass, and Volume

LET US LEARN ABOUT LENGTH, MASS, AND VOLUME

What is the correct unit to measure these objects? Circle your answer.

1.   cm   m

3.   g   kg

2.  cm   m

4.   ml   l

5. Use the ruler to measure the pencil.

cm

Change these units of measurement.

6. 700 centimetres

metres

7. 6 kilogram

grams

8. 14 litres

millilitres

9. 8000 millilitres

litres

10. 84 metres

centimetres

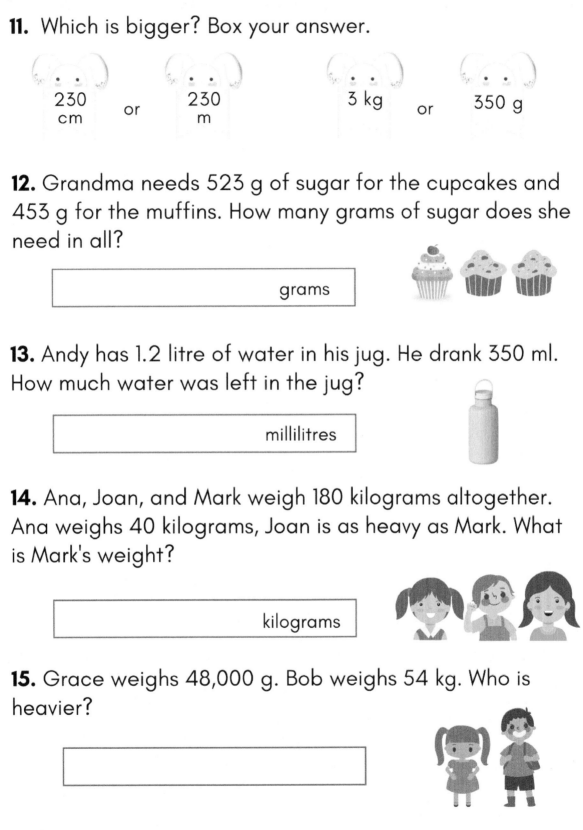

11. Which is bigger? Box your answer.

230 cm   or   230 m   3 kg   or   350 g

12. Grandma needs 523 g of sugar for the cupcakes and 453 g for the muffins. How many grams of sugar does she need in all?

grams

13. Andy has 1.2 litre of water in his jug. He drank 350 ml. How much water was left in the jug?

millilitres

14. Ana, Joan, and Mark weigh 180 kilograms altogether. Ana weighs 40 kilograms, Joan is as heavy as Mark. What is Mark's weight?

kilograms

15. Grace weighs 48,000 g. Bob weighs 54 kg. Who is heavier?

"I can convert, add, and subtract length, mass, and volume.."

Measuring Perimeter

LET US LEARN ABOUT PERIMETER

1. Find the perimeter of the triangle.

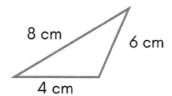

cm

2. A square measures 10 m on one side. What is the perimeter?

m

3. A shape measures 5 mm on each side. Find its perimeter.

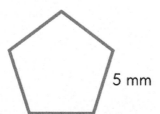

mm

4. Draw a rectangle with a perimeter of 18 cm.

1 box = 1 cm

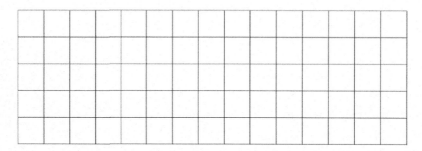

"I can measure the perimeter of 2D shapes."

Adding and Subtracting Money

LET US LEARN ABOUT MONEY

1. Karina has 57 pence. She bought a chocolate bar for 35 pence. How much does she have left?

pence

2. A book costs £12.50 and a bag costs £20.11. How much money is needed to buy these things?

£

3. Janina bought sweets for 25 pence and a fruit juice for 35 pence. If she had £ 1, how much has she got left?

pence

Patrick has £10 and he is planning to buy fruits. Here is the shopping list.

Apples	£ 3.20
Strawberries	£ 1.90
Pears	£ 3
Raspberries	£ 1
Cherries	£ 2

4. Does he have enough money to buy all the fruits in the list?

5. How much more money does he need?

"I can add and subtract money.."

Augmented Reality Page

TELLING THE TIME VIDEO PAGE

1) Go to **Chapter 5 ➤ Telling the time** in the app

2) **Move your phone** over the picture below

Don't cut out

Telling The Time

Telling Time

LET US TELL THE TIME

1. Write the time.

2. Write the time in words.

3. Circle the correct time.

   10:00 am

10:00 pm

   11:15 am

11:15 pm

4. James sleeps at 9:00 pm. He wakes up at 6:00 am. How many hours did he sleep?

| hours |

Solving Time Problems

LET US SOLVE TIME PROBLEMS

1. Andrew finished the Maths drill in 3 minutes. How many seconds did it take for him to finish the drill?

seconds

2. How many days does February have in a leap year?

days

3. The teacher gave homework on June 23rd which is due in 7 days. When is the deadline of the homework?

4. A train leaves at 8:20 am. After 45 minutes, it arrives at its destination. What time did it arrive?

Here is the schedule of store hours during the week.

Store Hours

Monday 8:00 – 5:00 pm
Tuesday 9:00 – 5:30 pm
Wednesday 8:00 – 5:00 pm
Thursday 9:00 – 5:30 pm
Friday 10:00 am – 7:00 pm

5. For how long is the store open on Friday?

hours

6. On Tuesday, Amy went to the shop at 8:35. How long does she have to wait until the store opens?

minutes

"I can solve problems involving time."

74

CHAPTER TEST

1. Complete the statement. Write mm, cm, or m.

A needle is about 30 [＿＿＿] long.

A house is about 7 [＿＿＿] tall.

A school bus is about 10 [＿＿＿] long.

A shoe box is about 25 [＿＿＿] long.

2. How long is the bamboo stick in mm?

[＿＿＿＿＿] mm

3. Change these units of measurement.

14 metres [＿＿＿＿ centimetres]

90 centimetres [＿＿＿＿ millimeters]

25 litres [＿＿＿＿ millilitres]

7000 grams [＿＿＿＿ kilograms]

4. Find the perimeter of a regular pentagon that measures 5 cm on one side.

[＿＿＿＿＿ cm]

5 cm

5. If the perimeter of a square is 36 m, how long is each side in cm?

36 m	? m

	cm

6. Ella bought a cupcake for 53 pence and a milkshake for 42 pence. How much did she spend in all?

	pence

7. Ben bought 2 kg of apples for £5 and 1 kg of cherries for £2. If he had £10, How much does he have left?

£

8. Tell the time.

9. How many minutes are there in 5 hours?

	minutes

10. Annie went to school at 8:00 am and came back home at 3:30 pm. How long did she stay in school?

hours	minutes

Augmented Reality Page

CHALLENGE QUESTIONS

1) Go to **Chapter 5 - Challenge** in the app
2) **Move your phone** over the cards below

Don't cut out

Measurement

Question

1

Measurement

Answer

1

Don't cut out

Measurement

Question

2

Measurement

Answer

2

Measurement

Question

3

Measurement

Answer

3

CERTIFICATE

THIS IS PRESENTED TO

For learing about Measurement

Using Tables

1. Look at the picture and complete the tally chart. The first one has been done for you.

Animal	Tally	Frequency
Frog	II	2
Bird		
Dog		
Cat		

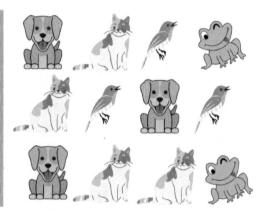

2. Look at the table about the colour of cars that passed by the school.

Color	Tally	Frequency
Red	II	2
White	IIII	5
Grey	IIII III	8

What is the colour of most cars?

How many cars passed by the school in total?

cars

3. Create a table about the favorite sports of Year 3 pupils.

Sport	Tally	Frequency

Tennis Tennis Football
Football Football Tennis
Cricket Football Cricket
Cricket Football Tennis
Tennis Cricket Football

"I can interpret and present data using tables."

Augmented Reality Page

BAR GRAPH AND PICTOGRAM

1) Go to **Chapter 6 Graph video** in the app
2) **Move your phone** over the picture below

Don't cut out

Interpreting Bar Charts

LET US INTERPRET BAR CHARTS

This is a bar chart about the number of tennis players from Year 1-6. Answer the following questions.

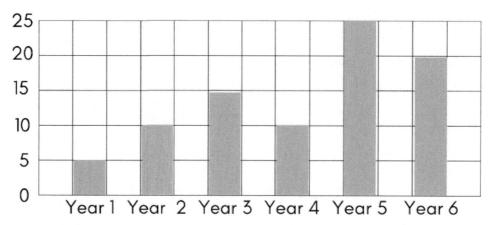

1. How many tennis players are there in Year 1?

players

2. What two years have the same amount of tennis players?

3. What year has the highest number of tennis players?

4. How many tennis players are there from Year 4 to Year 6?

players

5. How many more tennis players are there in Year 5 than in Year 3?

players

6. Create a bar chart about the insects that Lea saw in the garden. Use the data in the table. A sample is done for you.

Insect	Frequency
bees	7
beetles	4
butterflies	5
dragonflies	3

Insects that Lea saw in the Garden

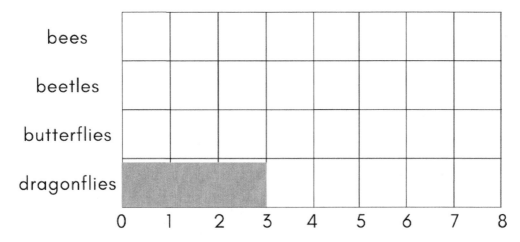

7. How many more butterflies are there than dragonflies?

butterflies

8. How many insects did Lea see in the garden altogether?

insects

"I can interpret and present data in a bar chart."

Interpreting Pictograms

LET US INTERPRET PICTOGRAMS

The pictogram shows the favourite colours of Year 3 pupils.

red	👤 👤 👤 👤 👤
blue	👤 👤 👤
green	👤 👤 👤 👤 👤 👤 👤
yellow	👤 👤 👤 👤 👤 👤 👤 👤 👤 👤 👤

👤 = 2 pupils

1. What colour is the least favourite?

2. How many pupils like red?

pupils

3. What color is the most popular?

4. How many more pupils like yellow than blue?

pupils

5. How many pupils voted for their favourite colour?

pupils

6. The pupils voted for the most popular desserts in the cafeteria. Complete the pictogram using the data from the table. The first one has been done for you.

cheesecake	9
apple pie	6
strawberry shortcake	18
red velvet cake	15

Popular Desserts in the Cafeteria

cheesecake	🍰 🍰 🍰
apple pie	
strawberry shortcake	
red velvet cake	

🍰 = 3 votes

7. What is the most popular dessert?

8. How many more pupils voted for apple pie than red velvet cake?

pupils

"I can interpret and present data in pictogram."

CHAPTER TEST

1. The table and pictogram show the favourite breakfast of Year 3 pupils. Complete the table. 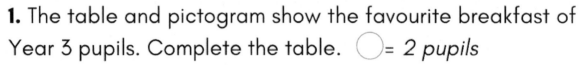 = *2 pupils*

Cereal	ЖЖ ЖЖ	
Crumpets	ЖЖ	
Toast	II	
Muffins	ЖЖ III	

Cereal	◯◯◯◯◯
Crumpets	◯◯◖
Toast	◯
Muffins	◯◯◯◯

2. How many chose cereal and muffins?

pupils

3. What is the most popular breakfast?

4. What is the least popular breakfast?

5. How many more chose crumpets than toast?

pupils

6. Complete the bar chart using the data above.

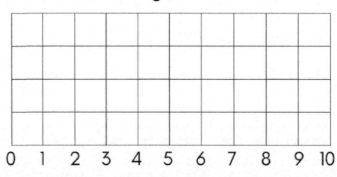

Augmented Reality Page

CHALLENGE QUESTIONS

1) Go to **Chapter 6 ➤ Challenge** in the app
2) **Move your phone** over the cards below

Don't cut out

Statistics

Question

1

Statistics

Answer

1

Don't cut out

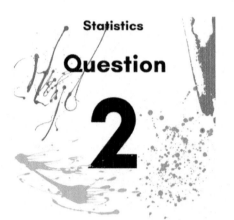

Statistics

Question

2

Statistics

Answer

2

Statistics

Question

3

Statistics

Answer

3

CERTIFICATE

THIS IS PRESENTED TO

○————————————————————○

For learning about Statistics

BELIEVE IN YOURSELF

OBJECTIVE TEST

LET US TEST WHAT YOU LEARNED THIS YEAR

1. Allan has 5 baskets with 8 bananas each. How many bananas does he have in all?

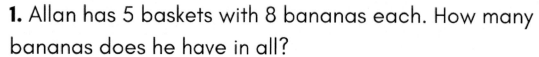

| bananas |

2. What is the value of 8 in 895?

3. Write 548 in words?

4. What number is represented by the grids?

5. Use >, <, and = to compare the numbers.

| 320 + 24 | | 300 + 44 | 290 - 150 | | 80 + 60 |
| 500 + 38 | | 570 - 8 | 635 + 200 | | 500 + 400 |

6. Add/subtract the numbers.

428	607	500	870
+335	+ 281	– 150	– 370

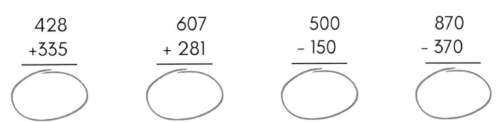

7. Lea has 100 gummy bears. She shared them equally with her 10 classmates. How many gummy bears did each classmate receive?

gummy bears

8. State an equivalent fraction to $\frac{1}{4}$ that has 12 as the denominator.

9. What is $\frac{3}{5}$ of 45?

10. If you will arrange $\frac{2}{11}$, $\frac{1}{5}$, $\frac{1}{3}$ from biggest to smallest, which would come first?

11. There are nine fruits in the basket. Four-ninths of the fruits are pears, two-ninths are grapes, and the rest are apples. What fraction of the fruits are apples?

12. What 3D shape has two circular bases and a curve surface?

> [   ]

13. Kate studies for 45 minutes a day. How many minutes does she spend studying for 5 days?

> [minutes]

14. Peter uses a balance scale to weigh vegetables. The potato weighs 2 kg. How many grams of carrots does he need to balance the scale?

> [grams]

15. Jacob saves £2 a week. How much will he save for 8 weeks?

> [£   ]

This pictogram shows the number of absentees in a week.

Year 1	◯ ◯ ◯
Year 2	◯ ◯ ◖
Year 3	◯ ◖

◯ = 2 absentees

16. How many absentees are there in Year 2?

> [absentees]

17. What is the total number of absentees from Year 1 to Year 3?

> [absentees]

ANSWER KEY

CHAPTER 1
Counting in Multiples

Q1. 4 **8** 12 **16** 20

Q2.

700	64	300	40	900	32	85
38	200	108	72	80	56	600

Q3. **250** carrots

Q4. **48, 24, 8**

Q5. **57 + 43**

10 and 100 More or Less of a Number

Q1.

Number	10 Less	10 More	100 Less	100 More
120	110	130	20	220
375	**365**	**385**	**275**	**475**
540	**530**	**550**	**440**	**640**
680	**670**	**690**	**580**	**780**

Q2.

100 less than 437 is greater than 400

100 more than 511 is greater than 700

10 more than 961 is the same as 971

Q3. 96 sticks

Place Value and Value

Q1.

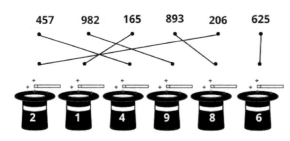

457   982   165   893   206   625

2   1   4   9   8   6

Q2.

Number	Place Value	Value
3<u>2</u>4	tens	20
48<u>5</u>	ones	5
<u>5</u>92	hundreds	500
<u>7</u>16	hundreds	700

Q3. 9 ones, 6 tens, 2 hundreds   **269**

7 hundreds, 8 tens, 3 ones   **783**

4 tens, 5 hundreds, 6 ones   **546**

Q4. 217= **200 + 10 + 7**

934= **900 + 30 + 4**

562= **500 + 60 + 2**

Q5. 875

Q6. 536

Comparing and Ordering Numbers

Q1.

329   ✗   368 ✓   623   809

Q2. 580 < 850   273 > 237   899 < 901

496 > 469   5+11 = 15+1   7+5 > 9-6

Q3. 99 cm - 107 cm - 152 cm

Representing Numbers

Q1. 28 votes

Q2. 4 cm

Q3. 268

Q4. 150 - 250 - 300

Q5. 648

Reading and Writing Numbers

Q1. 457 • three hundred forty-six

932 • four hundred fifty-seven

346 • six hundred eighty-one

681 • nine hundred thirty-two

Q2. 649 - **six hundred and forty-nine**

138 - **one hundred and thirty-eight**

725 - **seven hundred and twenty-five**

ANSWER KEY

Q3. ☹
    ☺
    ☺

Q4. fourteen years old

Solving Number Problems

Q1. 389

Q2. 73 kg

Q3. six hundred and forty-eight

Q4. **>**

    =

    >

Q5. 600

Q6. 856

Q7. 254

CHAPTER TEST

Q1. 250, 350, 450, 750

Q2. 863
    590

Q3. 4 hundreds, 30 tens, 5 ones

Q4. 780 - **700**   279 - **70**
    127 - **7**   724 - **700**

Q5. 700 + 50   =   750 + 0
    300 + 60   <   570 + 2
    620 + 5   >   420 + 5
    900 + 25   >   400 + 72
    150 + 8   =   100 + 58
    540 + 100 <   750 - 100

Q6. ✔ 100   150   300   450
    ✘ 984   948   894   849
    ✘ 675   672   653   638

Q7. **253 - 325 - 352 - 523 - 532**

Q8. 326
    243

Q9.
528 • — • six hundred and thirty-two
907 • — • nine hundred and seven
165 • — • five hundred twenty-eight
632 • — • two hundred and forty-three
      • one hundred and sixty-five

CHAPTER 2

Adding Mentally

Q1. 780 + 4 = **784**   520 + 60 = **580**
     320 + 500 = **820**   135 + 400 = **535**

Q2. 260 + **300** = 560   720 + **8** = 728
    605 + 90 = 695   **64** + 800 = 864

Q3. 594

Q4. 60, 20, 100

Subtracting Mentally

Q1. 350

Q2. 680 - 200 = **480**   920 - 80 = **840**
    750 - 5 = **745**   487 - 380 = **107**

Q3.
    173 - 23   280 - 110   965 - 60   329 - 329

Q4. 772 and 200

Written Addition

Q1. 600 + 376 = **976**   345 + 262 = **607**
    248 + 453 = **701**   568 + 402 = **970**
    536 + 249 = **785**   365 + 439 = **804**
    190 + 627 = **817**   752 + 143 = **895**

Q2. 264 + **322** = 586
    750 + 120 = 870
    539 + 243 = **782**

ANSWER KEY

LET US CHECK YOUR ANSWERS

Q3. **389** treats

Written Subtraction

Q1. 876 - 203 = **673**   698 - 325 = **373**

590 - 349 = **241**   794 - 581 = **213**

485 - 253 = **232**

Q2.

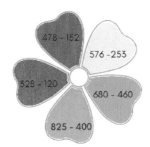

Q3. **145** metres

The 3, 4, and 8 Times Tables

Q1. 7 x 8 = **56**   3 x 9 = **27**   4 x 8 = **32**

4 x 10 = **40**   8 x 5 = **40**   3 x 4 = **12**

6 x 3 = **18**   7 x 4 = **28**   9 x 4 = **36**

Q2. 64, 56, 32, 80

Q3. 16, 28, 32, 8, 20, 36

Q4. 56 ÷ 8 = **7**   20 ÷ **4** = 5   **24** ÷ 3 = 8

Q5. **9** bones

Multiplying and Dividing Numbers

Q1. 2 x 3 x 5 = **30**   34 x 6 = **204**

6 x 50 = **300**   9 x 1 x 2 = **18**

20 x 5 = **100**   5 x 3 x 0 = **0**

7 x 2 x 2 = **28**   25 x 8 = **200**

8 x 50 = **400**

Q2. 12 ÷ 6 = **2** 72 ÷ 9 = **8** 450 ÷ 5 = **90**

Q3. Solution: **160 ÷ 8 = 20**

Answer: **20** candies

Estimating and Checking

Q1. 670 [**700**]   442 [**400**]
    - 238 [**200**]   + 590 [**600**]
         [**500**]   [**1000**]

Q2. 345 + 100 = 445

Q3. **88 ÷ 8 = 11 or 88 ÷ 11 = 8**

140 ÷ 7 = 20 or 140 ÷ 20 = 7

60 ÷ 4 = 15 or 60 ÷ 15 = 4

Q4. No since 11 x 10 = 110

Solving Computation Problems

Q1. **562** books

Q2. **168** pages

Q3. **90** marbles

Q4. **933**

Q5. **7** students

Q6. **70** litres

Q7. **180** minutes

Q8. **8** cookies

Q9. biggest 3-digit number   **853**

smallest 3-digit number - **358**

difference   **495**

CHAPTER TEST

Q1. 340 + 300 •   • 709
    930 - 220 •   • 230
    680 - 450 •   • 672
    542 + 130 •   • 710
    769 - 60 •   • 640

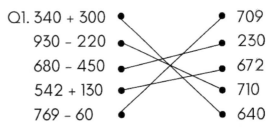

Q2. 530 + 259 = **789**

285 + 174 = **459**

406 + 583 = **989**

623 - 326 = **297**

768 - 158 = **610**

ANSWER KEY

Q3. 3 – **9** and **15**

    4 – **8** and **20**

    8 – **24** and **32**

Q4. 25 x 8 = **200**   120 ÷ 2 = **60**

    60 x 4 = **240**   64 ÷ 4 = **16**

    48 x 3 = **144**   90 ÷ 3 = **30**

Q5.
498	500		375	400
+ 180	200		+ 439	400
	300			800

663	700
– 349	300
	400

Q6.

569 + 219 = 788   **788 – 219 = 569** ✓

925 – 545 = 300   **300 + 545 = 845** ✗

10 x 8 = 40   **80 ÷ 10 = 8** ✓

144 ÷ 4 = 35   **35 x 4 = 140** ✗

Q7. **255** pencils

Q8. **5** toy cars

Q9. **150** minutes

CHAPTER 3

Counting in Tenths

Q1. $\frac{\mathbf{2}}{\mathbf{10}}$ – $\frac{\mathbf{5}}{\mathbf{10}}$ – $\frac{\mathbf{7}}{\mathbf{10}}$

Q2. 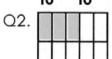 $\frac{3}{10}$ 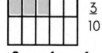 $\frac{9}{10}$

Q3. $\frac{\mathbf{3}}{\mathbf{10}}$ – $\frac{\mathbf{4}}{\mathbf{10}}$ – $\frac{\mathbf{6}}{\mathbf{10}}$ – $\frac{\mathbf{7}}{\mathbf{10}}$ – $\frac{\mathbf{8}}{\mathbf{10}}$

Q4. $\frac{\mathbf{4}}{\mathbf{10}}$

Equivalent Fractions

Q1. $\frac{4}{8}$

   $\frac{3}{6}$ 3 slices of pizza should be drawn.

Q2. Possible answers are:

$\frac{1}{4} = \frac{3}{12}$ $\frac{2}{4} = \frac{6}{12}$ $\frac{3}{4} = \frac{9}{12}$ $\frac{4}{4} = \frac{12}{12}$

Q3. Possible answers are:

$\frac{1}{3} = \frac{2}{6}$ $\frac{2}{3} = \frac{4}{6}$ $\frac{3}{3} = \frac{6}{6}$

Q4. Circle $\frac{4}{16}$, $\frac{1}{4}$, $\frac{6}{24}$

Q5. $\frac{1}{2}$ – $\frac{2}{4}$ – $\frac{4}{8}$

Comparing and Ordering Fractions

Q1. Yellow – $\frac{2}{8}$ Green – $\frac{7}{8}$

Q2. $\frac{4}{15} < \frac{14}{15}$ $\frac{5}{6} > \frac{3}{6}$ $\frac{9}{12} = \frac{9}{12}$

   $\frac{1}{7} > \frac{1}{8}$ $\frac{1}{6} < \frac{1}{4}$ $\frac{1}{2} > \frac{1}{5}$

Q3. $\frac{1}{9}$ – $\frac{3}{9}$ – $\frac{4}{9}$ – $\frac{6}{9}$ – $\frac{8}{9}$

Q4. $\frac{1}{3}$ – $\frac{1}{6}$ – $\frac{1}{9}$ – $\frac{1}{8}$ – $\frac{1}{12}$

Q5. Tom

Q6. Circle $\frac{4}{15}$, $\frac{5}{15}$, $\frac{6}{15}$

Q7. $\frac{1}{6}$ or $\frac{2}{6}$

Q8. $\frac{1}{3}$

Q9. $\frac{4}{5}$ or $\frac{4}{5}$

Q10. $\frac{3}{4}$ or $\frac{5}{4}$ or $\frac{6}{4}$

Adding and Subtracting Fraction

Q1. $\frac{8}{10}$

Q2. $\frac{3}{8}$

Q3. $\frac{3}{16} + \frac{9}{16} = \frac{\mathbf{12}}{\mathbf{16}}$ $\frac{2}{7} + \frac{5}{7} = \frac{\mathbf{7}}{\mathbf{7}}$ $\frac{8}{13} + \frac{4}{13} = \frac{\mathbf{12}}{\mathbf{13}}$

Q4. $\dfrac{15}{20} - \dfrac{9}{20} = \dfrac{\mathbf{6}}{\mathbf{20}}$ $\dfrac{9}{10} - \dfrac{4}{10} = \dfrac{\mathbf{5}}{\mathbf{10}}$ $\dfrac{14}{15} - \dfrac{7}{15} = \dfrac{\mathbf{7}}{\mathbf{15}}$

Q5. $\dfrac{4}{9} + \dfrac{\mathbf{5}}{\mathbf{9}} = \dfrac{9}{9}$ $\dfrac{\mathbf{2}}{\mathbf{14}} + \dfrac{8}{14} = \dfrac{10}{14}$ $\dfrac{5}{6} - \dfrac{\mathbf{4}}{\mathbf{6}} = \dfrac{1}{6}$

Q6. $\dfrac{4}{8}$

Q7. $\dfrac{2}{9}$

Q8. $\dfrac{5}{7}$

Q9. $\dfrac{1}{5}$

Q10. $\dfrac{6}{8}$

Q11. $\dfrac{2}{8}$

Q12. $\dfrac{7}{10}$

Unit and Non-Unit Fraction

Q1. $\dfrac{1}{5}$ – $\dfrac{\mathbf{6}}{\mathbf{8}}$ – $\dfrac{1}{4}$

Q2. 2 cats should be boxed.

Q3. Circle $\dfrac{\mathbf{1}}{\mathbf{16}} \quad \dfrac{\mathbf{1}}{\mathbf{4}} \quad \dfrac{\mathbf{1}}{\mathbf{7}} \quad \dfrac{\mathbf{1}}{\mathbf{10}}$

     Cross $\dfrac{\mathbf{2}}{\mathbf{3}} \quad \dfrac{\mathbf{3}}{\mathbf{5}} \quad \dfrac{\mathbf{6}}{\mathbf{8}}$

Q4. 12 candies

Q5. 8 roses

Q6. 9 apples should be boxed.

Q7. $\dfrac{1}{2}$ of 12 = **6** $\dfrac{1}{6}$ of 48 = **8** $\dfrac{2}{5}$ of 45= **18**

     $\dfrac{1}{3}$ of 36 = **12** $\dfrac{3}{4}$ of 20 = **15** $\dfrac{2}{7}$ of 49= **14**

Q8. *30 should be circled.*

Q9. **18**

Q10. **90** cm

Q11. £**9**

Solving Fraction Problems

Q1. $\dfrac{2}{3}$

Q2. **20** marbles

Q3. **8** girls

Q4. **4** doughnuts

Q5. Dad

Q6. $\dfrac{2}{5}$

Q7. $\dfrac{6}{10}$

Q8. $\dfrac{4}{10}$

Q9. **36** tablecloths

CHAPTER TEST

Q1. $\dfrac{2}{10}$

Q2. $\dfrac{4}{10}$

Q3. $\dfrac{6}{10}$

Q4. $\dfrac{4}{5} - \dfrac{2}{6} - \dfrac{2}{3}$

Q5. **8** bars

Q6. *Circle* $\dfrac{4}{16}, \dfrac{2}{8}, \dfrac{3}{12}$

Q7. $\dfrac{1}{90} < \dfrac{1}{9}$ $\dfrac{1}{8} < \dfrac{1}{3}$ $\dfrac{9}{12} = \dfrac{9}{12}$

Q8. *Possible answers are:*
$\dfrac{8}{13} \quad \dfrac{9}{13} \quad \dfrac{10}{13} \quad \dfrac{11}{13} \quad \dfrac{12}{13} \quad \dfrac{13}{13}$

Q9. $\dfrac{2}{13} - \dfrac{4}{13} - \dfrac{5}{13} - \dfrac{8}{13} - \dfrac{10}{13}$

Q10. $\dfrac{6}{10} + \dfrac{\mathbf{3}}{\mathbf{10}} = \dfrac{9}{10}$ $\dfrac{7}{8} - \dfrac{\mathbf{3}}{\mathbf{8}} = \dfrac{4}{8}$

     $\dfrac{\mathbf{8}}{\mathbf{15}} + \dfrac{5}{15} = \dfrac{13}{15}$

Q11. $\dfrac{5}{6}$

Q12. $\dfrac{4}{6}$

CHAPTER 4

2D Shapes

Q1. circle

Q2. rectangle

Q3. triangle

Q4. square

ANSWER KEY

LET US CHECK YOUR ANSWERS

Q5.

Q6.

Q7. **4** sides

Q8. **3** sides

Q9. **5** sides

Q10. **8** sides

Q11. **4** sides

Q12. scalene

Q13. isosceles

Q14. scalene

Q15. equilateral

3D Shapes

Q1. cone

Q2. sphere

Q3. cuboid

Q4. cube

Q5. pyramid

Q6. cylinder

Q7.

Q8.

Cylinder ● → ● It has no flat surfaces.

Sphere ● → ● It has two circular bases and a curved surface.

Cube ● → ● It has six square faces.

Q9. Edges   **1**

    Faces   **2**

    Vertices   **1**

Q10. Edges   **8**

    Faces   **5**

    Vertices   **5**

Q11. Edges   **12**

    Faces   **6**

    Vertices   **8**

Q12. Edges   **2**

    Faces   **3**

    Vertices   **0**

Q13. cylinder

Q14. square based pyramid/ pyramid

Recognizing Angles

Q1. right

Q2. acute

Q3. obtuse

Q4. *Colour square, triangle, and rectangle*

Q5. RIGHT

    OBTUSE

    ACUTE

Q6. **4** right angles

Lines

Q1. **7** vertical lines

    7 horizontal lines

Q2. **H**

Q3. parallel

Q4. perpendicular

Q5. perpendicular

Q6. *(Red)* Parallel lines can meet eventually.

    (Green) Perpendicular lines always make a 90-degree angle.

ANSWER KEY

LET US CHECK YOUR ANSWERS

Q7. Side F

Q8. Side G, D

Q9. No

Q10.

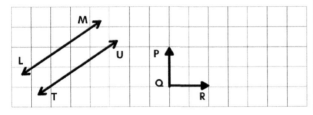

CHAPTER TEST

Q1.

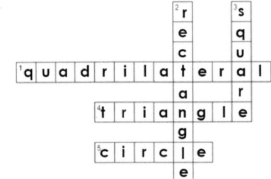

Q2.

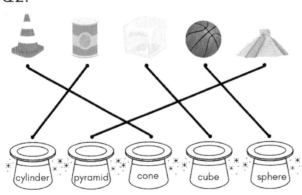

Q3. ✗ A circle is a 3D shape.

✓ A cone is composed of a circular base and an apex.

✗ A shape with 6 square faces is called a pyramid.

Q4.

Acute	Right	Obtuse
C	B	A
E	D	F

Q5. perpendicular

parallel

perpendicular

CHAPTER 5

Length, Mass, and Volume

Q1. cm

Q2. m

Q3. g

Q4. l

Q5. **7** cm

Q6. **7** metres

Q7. **6,000** grams

Q8. **14,000** millilitres

Q9. **8** litres

Q10. **8400** centimetres

Q11.

 or

Q12. **976** grams

Q13. **850** millilitres

Q14. **70** kilograms

Q15. Bob

Measuring Perimeter

Q1. **18** cm

Q2. **40** cm

Q3. **25** mm

ANSWER KEY

LET US CHECK YOUR ANSWERS

Q4.

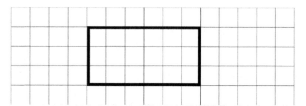

Adding and Subtracting Money

Q1. **22** pence
Q2. **£32.61**
Q3. **40** pence
Q4. **No**
Q5. **£1.10**

Telling Time

Q1. 3:30
8:00
10:45
1:20
Q2. three o'clock in the afternoon
nine fifty in the morning
Q3. *Circle 10:00 am*
Circle 11:15 pm
Q4. **9** hours

Solving Time Problems

Q1. **180** seconds
Q2. **29** days
Q3. **June 30th**
Q4. **9:05 am**
Q5. **9** hours
Q6. **25** minutes

CHAPTER TEST

Q1. mm
m
m
cm
Q2. 100 mm
Q3. **1400** centimetres
900 millimetres
25,000 millilitres
7 kilograms
Q4. **25** cm
Q5. **900** cm
Q6. **95** pence
Q7. **£3**
Q8. 3:00
4:40
9:10
10:45
Q9. **300** minutes
Q10. **7** hours **30** minutes

CHAPTER 6

Using Tables

Q1.

Animal	Tally	Frequency
Frog	II	2
Bird	III	3
Dog	III	3
Cat	IIII	4

ANSWER KEY

Q2. Grey

15 cars

Q3.

Sport	Tally	Frequency
Tennis	ЖHT	5
Football	ЖHT I	6
Cricket	IIII	4

Interpreting Bar Charts

Q1. **5** players

Q2. Year 2 and Year 4

Q3. Year 5

Q4. **55** players

Q5. **10** players

Q6.

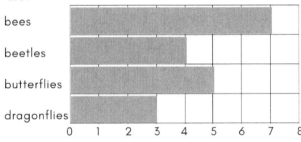

Q7. **2** butterflies

Q8. **19** insects

Interpreting Pictogram

Q1. blue

Q2. **10** pupils

Q3. yellow

Q4. **14** pupils

Q5. **50** pupils

Q6.

cheesecake	🍰 🍰 🍰
apple pie	🍰 🍰
strawberry shortcake	🍰 🍰 🍰 🍰 🍰 🍰
red velvet cake	🍰 🍰 🍰 🍰 🍰

Q7. strawberry shortcake

Q8. **9** pupils

CHAPTER TEST

Q1.

Cereal	ЖHT ЖHT	10
Crumpets	ЖHT	5
Toast	II	2
Muffins	ЖHT III	8

Q2. **18** pupils

Q3. Cereal

Q4. Toast

Q5. **3** pupils

Q6.

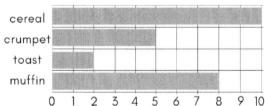

99

ANSWER KEY

LET US CHECK YOUR ANSWERS

OBJECTIVE TEST

Q1. 40 bananas

Q2. 800

Q3. five hundred and forty-eight

Q4. 359

Q5.
320 + 24	=	300 + 44
500 + 38	<	570 – 8
290 – 150	=	80 + 60
635 + 200	<	500 + 400

Q6.

428	607	500	870
+335	+ 281	– 150	– 370
763	**888**	**350**	**500**

Q7. **10** gummy bears

Q8. $\frac{3}{12}$

Q9. 27

Q10. $\frac{1}{3}$

Q11. $\frac{3}{9}$

Q12. cylinder

Q13. **225** minutes

Q14. **2,000** grams

Q15. **£16**

Q16. **5** absentees

Q17. **14** absentees

Extra Cut Out Cards

Multiples

Place Value

Place Value   Place Value

3   5

Place Value

7

Ordering and Comparing

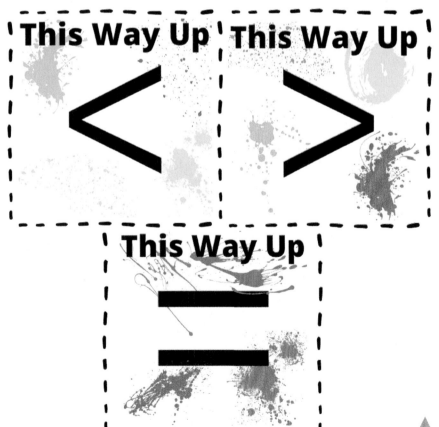

This Way Up   **This Way Up**

<   >

This Way Up

=

Addition and Subtraction

Addition and Subtraction

4

Addition and Subtraction

5

Addition and Subtraction

8

Addition and Subtraction

30

Addition and Subtraction

111

Addition and Subtraction

213

Addition and Subtraction

221

Addition and Subtraction

417

103

Addition and Subtraction

Addition and Subtraction

427

Addition and Subtraction

500

Addition and Subtraction

100

Addition and Subtraction

+

Addition and Subtraction

This Way Up

—

Addition and
Subtraction
Fraction

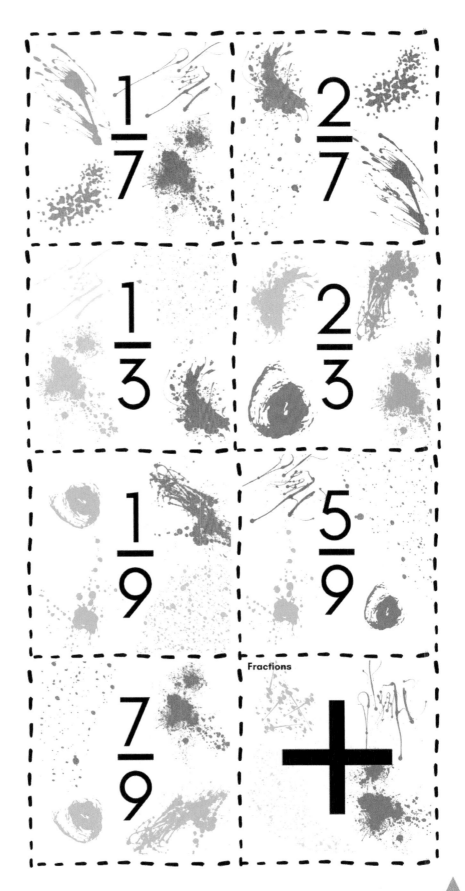

$\dfrac{1}{7}$

$\dfrac{2}{7}$

$\dfrac{1}{3}$

$\dfrac{2}{3}$

$\dfrac{1}{9}$

$\dfrac{5}{9}$

Fractions

$\dfrac{7}{9}$

$+$

Addition and
Subtraction
Fraction

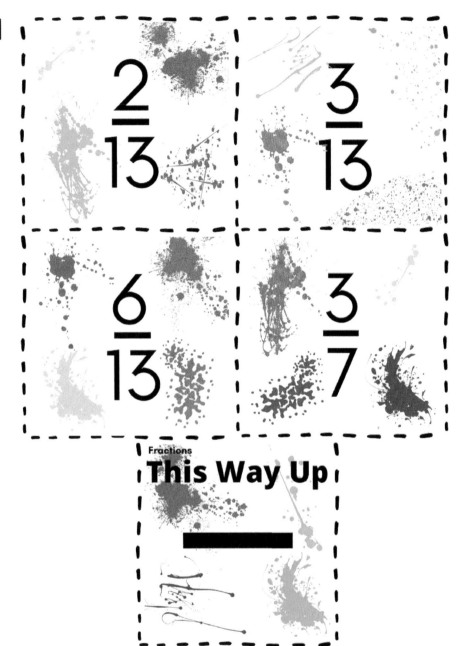

$$\frac{2}{13}$$

$$\frac{3}{13}$$

$$\frac{6}{13}$$

$$\frac{3}{7}$$

Fractions
This Way Up